GRANDPA,
TELL ME
ABOUT
THE TIME...

MEMORIES-IN-A-MINUTE
PROMPT JOURNAL

ISBN 13: 978-1-4621-4266-8

Published by Plain Sight Publishing, an imprint of Cedar Fort, Inc.,
2373 W. 700 S., Springville, UT 84663
Distributed by Cedar Fort, Inc., www.cedarfort.com

Cover and page design by Shawnda T. Craig
Cover design © 2022 by Cedar Fort, Inc.
Edited by Heather Holm

Printed in the United States

10 9 8 7 6 5 4 3 2 1

Printed on acid-free paper

GRANDPA,
TELL ME
ABOUT
THE TIME...

MEMORIES-IN-A-MINUTE
PROMPT JOURNAL

Plain Sight Publishing
An imprint of Cedar Fort, Inc.
Springville, Utah

CONTENTS

THIS BOOK BELONGS TO:

_____

INTRODUCTION

THE BEST THINGS IN LIFE are the people we love, the places we have been, and the memories we have made along the way.

Everyone loves to hear grandpa's stories. This simple, guided memory journal is a fun, practical way to document his life experiences and share his legacy for generations to come.

Keep his rich personal history all in one place and record his favorite memories using our unique "memories-in-a-minute" prompts.

FAMILY...

Where life begins,
& love never ends.

ONCE I WAS A CHILD

_____

FULL NAME

_____

BIRTHDATE

_____

BIRTHPLACE

Were you born in a hospital, at home, or elsewhere?

_____

_____

How much did you weigh when you were born?

_____

Do you have a unique or special birth story?

_____

_____

_____

_____

Were you named after anyone? _____

_____

_____

_____

How did your parents come up with your name? _____

_____

_____

_____

Did they agree on a name right away? _____

_____

_____

Did you have a nickname growing up? _____

_____

How did you get that nickname? _____

_____

_____

_____

_____

_____

Where did you grow up? _____

_____

_____

In a few words, describe your childhood home. _____

_____

_____

_____

_____

_____

_____

_____

_____

_____

_____

How many phones did your home have? _____

_____

_____

Did your home have indoor plumbing? _____

_____

_____

How many bathrooms were there? _____

_____

_____

What is your earliest memory? _____

_____

_____

_____

_____

_____

_____

_____

_____

_____

_____

_____

_____

_____

_____

_____

_____

_____

_____

_____

_____

_____

HOW MUCH
WAS YOUR ALLOWANCE?

WHAT DID YOU SPEND YOUR
ALLOWANCE ON MOST OFTEN?

DID YOU HAVE ANY PETS?

What were your favorite dishes your family liked to prepare?

_____

_____

_____

_____

_____

_____

_____

Was your life financially comfortable, or did your family struggle to have enough money? _____

_____

_____

_____

_____

_____

_____

Were you taught to pay cash for things or borrow for your needs?

_____

_____

_____

_____

Share one of the early birthday memories you had with your family.

_____

_____

_____

_____

_____

_____

_____

_____

_____

_____

_____

_____

_____

_____

_____

_____

_____

_____

_____

_____

_____

_____

_____

Did you share a bedroom with a sibling?

What kind of chores did you have to do as a kid?

How were you punished if you misbehaved?

Who did most of the cooking in your home? _____

_____

_____

_____

_____

_____

_____

Did you eat together as a family every night? _____

_____

_____

_____

_____

_____

_____

What is a food you loved as a child and still enjoy today?

_____

_____

_____

_____

_____

_____

_____

_____

Did you ever have a babysitter or nanny?

_____

_____

_____

What childhood activity did you enjoy that kids do not seem to enjoy today? _____

_____

_____

_____

_____

_____

_____

What did you do when you were home alone?

_____

_____

_____

_____

_____

_____

_____

_____

_____

Is there something from your childhood you wish was still popular today? _____

_____

_____

_____

_____

Did you ever sneak out of the house when you weren't supposed to? Where did you go? _____

_____

_____

_____

_____

_____

_____

What was the most significant problem you worried about when you were young? _____

_____

_____

_____

_____

_____

_____

_____

Who did you look up to as a child and why?

_____

_____

_____

_____

_____

Do you still admire them today?

_____

_____

_____

_____

What did you want to be when you grew up?

_____

_____

_____

How old were you when you moved out of your parents' home?

_____

_____

_____

What is a food you hated as a child, and how do you feel about it now?

_____

_____

_____

_____

Which was your favorite holiday and why? _____

_____

_____

_____

_____

_____

_____

Were you naughty or well-behaved? _____

_____

_____

_____

What mischievous act did you do when you were young? _____

_____

_____

_____

_____

WHAT WERE SOME OF YOUR FAVORITE PASTIMES?

Did you have a favorite toy? _____

When you were young, were you shy or outgoing, popular or average?

What scared you as a child? _____

Who were your childhood heroes?

What is your most embarrassing moment as a child?

What is one of the most significant hardships you had to endure as a child?

Anything special or unique you remember from your childhood that you want to share?

MY FAMILY TREE

GREAT GRANDPA

GREAT GRANDPA

GREAT GRANDMA

GREAT GRANDMA

GREAT GRANDPA

GREAT GRANDPA

GREAT GRANDMA

GREAT GRANDMA

GRANDPA (DAD'S DAD)

GRANDPA (MOM'S DAD)

GRANDMA (DAD'S MOM)

GRANDMA (MOM'S MOM)

DAD

MOM

ME

A little bit crazy,
a little bit loud,
a whole lot
OF LOVE.

MOM, DAD & THE KIDS

MOM'S NAME & BIRTHDATE

DAD'S NAME & BIRTHDATE

STEP PARENT'S NAME & BIRTHDATE

STEP PARENT'S NAME & BIRTHDATE

SIBLING'S NAME & BIRTHDATE

SIBLING'S NAME & BIRTHDATE

SIBLING'S NAME & BIRTHDATE

SIBLING'S NAME & BIRTHDATE

SIBLING'S NAME & BIRTHDATE

SIBLING'S NAME & BIRTHDATE

SIBLING'S NAME & BIRTHDATE

SIBLING'S NAME & BIRTHDATE

SIBLING'S NAME & BIRTHDATE

SIBLING'S NAME & BIRTHDATE

SIBLING'S NAME & BIRTHDATE

SIBLING'S NAME & BIRTHDATE

Were you raised in a household with both of your biological parents?

_____

_____

_____

_____

What is an essential life skill your parents taught you?

_____

_____

_____

_____

_____

_____

_____

Have you ever visited the home where your mom or dad lived as a

child? _____

_____

_____

_____

_____

_____

_____

_____

Where did your mom grow up?

Where was your mom's childhood home?

Was your mom a homemaker, or did she work outside the home?

What was your mom's occupation?

What do you remember most about your mom?

Where did your dad grow up? _____

_____

_____

Where was your dad's childhood home? _____

_____

_____

What was your dad's occupation? _____

_____

_____

_____

What would you like others to know about your dad?

_____

_____

_____

_____

_____

_____

_____

_____

_____

Did either of your parents serve in the military? If so, which branch? _____

_____

_____

_____

_____

What is the best advice your parents ever gave you?

_____

_____

_____

_____

_____

What was the best part of growing up with or without siblings? _____

_____

_____

_____

_____

_____

_____

_____

_____

How is your family different from other families? Why? _____

_____

_____

_____

_____

_____

_____

_____

How were birthdays celebrated in your family? _____

_____

_____

_____

_____

What were some of your favorite Halloween costumes you and your

siblings wore? _____

_____

_____

_____

_____

_____

HOW DID YOUR FAMILY
CELEBRATE THANKSGIVING?

WHAT ARE SOME OF THE THINGS YOUR FAMILY
WOULD DO TO CELEBRATE CHRISTMAS?

What are your siblings' names, and how much older/younger are they? _____

_____

_____

_____

_____

_____

Share one memory of each of your siblings. _____

_____

_____

_____

_____

_____

_____

_____

_____

_____

_____

_____

_____

_____

_____

_____

_____

Where did you go on your most memorable vacation with your
family? _____

_____

_____

_____

_____

_____

Did you ever travel abroad with your family? _____

_____

_____

_____

_____

Where were your family's regular vacation destinations? _____

_____

_____

_____

_____

_____

_____

Anything special or unique you remember about your parents
or your siblings you want to share? _____

_____

_____

_____

_____

_____

_____

_____

_____

_____

_____

_____

_____

_____

_____

_____

_____

_____

_____

_____

_____

Like the branches
on a tree, our

FAMILY grows in

different directions,

yet our roots remain

AS ONE.

THE REST OF US

GRANDMOTHER'S FULL NAME

GRANDMOTHER'S BIRTHDATE & BIRTHPLACE

GRANDFATHER'S FULL NAME

GRANDFATHER'S BIRTHDATE & BIRTHPLACE

GRANDMOTHER'S FULL NAME

GRANDMOTHER'S BIRTHDATE & BIRTHPLACE

GRANDFATHER'S FULL NAME

GRANDFATHER'S BIRTHDATE & BIRTHPLACE

Describe what you know about each of your grandmas and grandpas.

_____
_____
_____
_____
_____
_____
_____
_____
_____
_____
_____
_____
_____
_____
_____
_____
_____
_____
_____
_____
_____
_____
_____

BEYOND YOUR IMMEDIATE
FAMILY MEMBERS, WHICH
OTHER MEMBERS OF YOUR
FAMILY DID YOU SEE OFTEN?

DID YOU SPEND A LOT OF TIME WITH YOUR EXTENDED FAMILY?

Where do most of your relatives live today? _____

_____

_____

_____

_____

_____

Which countries are your relatives from initially? _____

_____

_____

_____

_____

_____

Who is the oldest family member you remember? _____

_____

_____

_____

_____

_____

What family stories did your grandma/grandpa share with you about their lives? _____

_____

_____

_____

_____

_____

_____

_____

_____

_____

_____

_____

_____

_____

_____

FIRST TIME FOR EVERYTHING

MILESTONES

List the dates and details for each experience below.

Job _____

Crush _____

Kiss _____

Date _____

Heartbreak _____

Pet _____

Car _____

Movie _____

School _____

Concert _____

Home (year & cost) _____

Plane ride _____

Big trip without your parents _____

Tattoo _____

Piercing _____

Proposal _____

Engagement _____

Marriage _____

True love _____

Child _____

MY BUCKET LIST

List the top ten things you would have on your bucket list.

If you want to make

a difference in the

world, you must

BE DIFFERENT

from the world.

MY WORLD

WHEN YOU WERE YOUNG . . .

How much did bread cost? _____

_____

How much did milk cost? _____

_____

How much did stamps cost? _____

_____

How much did gas cost? _____

_____

How much did a movie ticket cost? _____

_____

How much did a candy bar cost? _____

_____

What were prices of other items you remember?

_____

_____

_____

Do you think life is easier or harder for kids these days compared to your childhood? _____

_____

_____

_____

_____

_____

_____

_____

_____

Did you live during a major war? If so, what do you remember during that time? _____

_____

_____

_____

_____

_____

_____

_____

_____

_____

_____

_____

What single invention has had the most significant impact on your life?

_____

_____

_____

_____

_____

_____

_____

Who would you like to meet in person if you had the chance?

_____

_____

_____

_____

_____

Have you ever met someone famous? Who? _____

_____

_____

_____

_____

_____

_____

_____

What is the biggest problem you see in the world today?

Did you serve in the military? Which branch?

What was a significant event that happened in the world that you vividly remember?

Which United States President was in office during your youth that you can remember? _____

_____

_____

_____

_____

What was the most significant technological advancement that occurred in your lifetime? _____

_____

_____

_____

_____

_____

_____

_____

Have advancements in technology changed your life for better or for worse? _____

_____

_____

_____

_____

_____

_____

Remembering the world around you as a youth, is there anything special or unique you want to share? _____

_____

_____

_____

_____

_____

_____

_____

_____

_____

_____

_____

_____

_____

_____

_____

_____

_____

_____

_____

_____

_____

WORKING HARD

EVERY JOB I HAVE EVER HAD

(company name/position/pay)

WHEELS
VEHICLES I HAVE OWNED OR DRIVEN

(Year/Make/Model)

Don't dream of success.

WORK FOR IT.

EARNING A LIVING

When you were growing up, what was your dream job and why? _____

_____

_____

_____

_____

What was the first job you ever had? _____

_____

_____

What was the best job you ever had and why? _____

_____

_____

_____

_____

_____

_____

HOW DID YOU
CHOOSE YOUR CAREER?

Which job would you never want to have again? Why?

_____

_____

_____

Why do you work where you do? _____

_____

_____

_____

What do you do well in your occupation? _____

_____

_____

_____

Would you say that you work harder or smarter? _____

_____

_____

_____

_____

What education or training did you need to gain to do your work?

_____

_____

_____

_____

_____

What knowledge did you learn on the job that you never expected to

learn? _____

_____

_____

_____

_____

_____

_____

_____

_____

_____

_____

List some of your most significant accomplishments in your
career. _____

_____

_____

_____

_____

_____

What's the most important thing you need to do to be
successful in a career? _____

_____

_____

_____

_____

_____

If you could start over, which career would you like to have?

_____

_____

_____

_____

_____

_____

_____

_____

What has helped you succeed most at work? _____

_____

_____

_____

_____

_____

What is the most challenging part of your job? _____

_____

_____

_____

_____

Which tool do you use the most at work? _____

_____

_____

_____

_____

What characteristics do you look for in a good employee?

_____

_____

_____

_____

_____

_____

_____

Anything special or unique you remember about work or earning a living that you want to share? _____

_____

_____

_____

_____

_____

_____

_____

_____

_____

_____

_____

_____

_____

_____

_____

_____

_____

_____

_____

_____

_____

Far from what
I once was,
but not yet
what I am
GOING TO BE.

LEARNING & STRETCHING

Was education valued in your home? If so, in what ways were
you encouraged to succeed? _____

_____

_____

_____

_____

_____

_____

_____

_____

_____

_____

_____

_____

_____

_____

_____

_____

_____

_____

_____

Which schools did you attend? _____

_____

_____

_____

_____

_____

What did you do during recess at school? _____

_____

_____

_____

_____

Did you win any awards when you attended school? _____

_____

_____

_____

_____

_____

Did you have a favorite teacher? _____

_____

_____

_____

WHAT IS YOUR
FAVORITE MEMORY
FROM YOUR SCHOOL DAYS?

WERE YOU EVER CALLED TO THE
PRINCIPAL'S OFFICE? WHY?

Did you ever receive detention or other school punishments? _____

_____

_____

_____

_____

How did you travel to and from school? _____

_____

_____

_____

_____

Were you ever bullied in school? If so, what did you do?

_____

_____

_____

_____

Share a memory you have from your school days.

_____

_____

_____

_____

What was your best subject at school? _____

_____

_____

_____

_____

What was your least favorite subject at school?

_____

_____

_____

_____

Did you participate in any extracurricular activities?

_____

_____

_____

_____

_____

_____

Were you in any clubs in high school? _____

_____

_____

_____

Who taught you to drive? _____

_____

_____

_____

Did you ever attend any school dances? Which was your most memorable and why? _____

_____

_____

_____

_____

_____

_____

_____

Did you ever skip school? How old were you, and what did you do instead? _____

_____

_____

_____

_____

_____

_____

_____

What year did you graduate from high school?

_____

_____

How many people were in your graduating class?

_____

_____

What is the highest level of education you achieved?

_____

_____

_____

_____

Did you attend college or receive any technical
training after high school? Where did you go?
What did you study? _____

_____

_____

_____

_____

_____

_____

_____

We didn't know we
were making memories.
We just knew we were
HAVING FUN.

FRIENDS

Who was your best friend in elementary school?

_____

_____

_____

In middle school? _____

_____

_____

In high school? _____

_____

_____

Do you still stay in touch with any of your childhood
friends? _____

_____

_____

_____

_____

WHO ARE YOUR CLOSEST FRIENDS TODAY?

How do you maintain this relationship? _____

_____

_____

_____

_____

Who is your oldest friend? Share a memory you had with them.

_____

_____

_____

_____

_____

_____

_____

What kinds of things do you like to do when you are together?

_____

_____

_____

_____

_____

_____

_____

_____

_____

_____

What traits do you value most in a friend? _____

_____

_____

_____

_____

_____

_____

_____

_____

_____

_____

_____

Share some stories of the adventures you have had with your friends.

_____

_____

_____

_____

_____

_____

_____

_____

_____

_____

_____

_____

_____

_____

_____

_____

_____

_____

_____

_____

_____

_____

_____

WOULD YOU RATHER . . .
(circle your answer)

Always be late OR always be early?

Movies OR music?

Candy OR cake?

Unlimited tacos for life OR unlimited sushi for life?

Save money OR spend money?

Set the table for dinner OR clean up after dinner?

Sleep in OR wake up early?

Have more time OR have more money?

Fiction OR nonfiction?

Have world peace OR stop world hunger?

Be an adult your whole life OR be a kid your whole life?

Large crowd OR small group?

Brand new house OR brand new car?

Hot weather OR cold weather?

Be a dancer OR be a singer?

Ocean OR mountains?

Cheeseburger OR fine dining?

Watch a scary movie OR watch a comedy?

Chocolate OR vanilla?

WOULD YOU RATHER . . .
(circle your answer)

Read a book OR watch TV?

Barefoot OR shoes?

Talk OR text?

Be invisible OR read minds?

Rewind time OR pause time?

Shower OR bath?

Winter OR summer?

Rain OR sunshine?

Always lose OR never play?

Salty OR sweet?

Drive fast OR drive slow?

Spicy food OR not spicy food?

Optimist OR pessimist?

Live in the city OR live in the country?

Clean OR messy?

Spontaneity OR planned?

Cats OR dogs?

Time with others OR time alone?

Walking OR riding a bike?

The beautiful thing about

YOUNG LOVE

is the truth we believed in

OUR HEARTS

that it would last forever.

BOY MEETS GIRL

Who was your first crush? _____
_____
_____

How old were you when you had your first crush?
_____

What attracted you to her? _____
_____
_____
_____

How old were you when you had your first kiss?
_____
_____

Who did you share your first kiss with, and where did it
happen? _____
_____
_____
_____
_____

Did your family have dating rules? _____

_____

_____

_____

_____

_____

How old were you when you went on your first date?

Who was it with, and what did you do? _____

_____

_____

_____

_____

_____

_____

_____

_____

_____

_____

_____

_____

_____

_____

Share one of your most memorable dates. Where did you go, and
with whom? _____

_____

_____

_____

_____

_____

_____

_____

_____

_____

_____

_____

_____

_____

_____

_____

_____

_____

_____

_____

_____

_____

_____

HOW OLD WERE YOU
WHEN YOU HAD YOUR FIRST
REAL GIRLFRIEND?

Have you ever broken someone's heart? _____

_____

_____

_____

_____

_____

_____

_____

_____

_____

_____

_____

Share something embarrassing that happened to you on a date.

Anything special or unique you remember about your love life or
relationships that you want to share? _____

_____

_____

_____

_____

_____

_____

_____

_____

_____

_____

_____

_____

_____

_____

_____

_____

_____

_____

_____

_____

_____

_____

I'm so happy that

YOU'RE MINE.

FALLING IN LOVE

_____

SPOUSE'S FULL NAME

_____

SPOUSE'S BIRTHDATE & BIRTHPLACE

_____

MARRIAGE DATE

_____

MARRIAGE PLACE

WHAT IS ONE WORD THAT DESCRIBES YOUR FIRST KISS?

How did you and your spouse meet? _____

_____

_____

_____

_____

Where did you go on your first date? _____

_____

_____

_____

_____

When did you know you wanted to get married?

_____

_____

_____

_____

_____

_____

_____

_____

_____

_____

_____

_____

_____

How long was it from the time you met until you were married?

_____

_____

_____

_____

How long were you engaged? _____

_____

_____

_____

How did you propose to your spouse or how did your spouse propose
to you? _____

_____

_____

_____

_____

_____

_____

_____

_____

_____

_____

_____

_____

_____

_____

_____

_____

_____

_____

_____

Describe your wedding day. _____

_____

_____

_____

_____

_____

_____

_____

_____

_____

_____

_____

_____

_____

_____

_____

_____

_____

_____

_____

_____

_____

_____

What do you love most about your spouse? _____

_____

_____

_____

_____

_____

_____

What was the most challenging part about going from
single life to being married? _____

_____

_____

_____

_____

_____

What advice would you give your grandchildren about
marriage? _____

_____

_____

_____

_____

What is the key to being happy in a marriage?

_____
_____
_____
_____
_____
_____
_____

What do you wish you had known before you got
married? _____
_____
_____
_____
_____
_____
_____

When you initially met your spouse, what did you think?
_____
_____
_____
_____

Who initiated your first kiss? How and where did it happen?

What feature of your spouse were you attracted to initially?

What have you grown to appreciate most about your spouse?

What is the best way your spouse shows you they love you?

Where is your favorite place to spend time together?

_____

_____

_____

_____

What was the best gift you have ever received?

_____

_____

_____

_____

What is something your spouse does exceptionally well?

_____

_____

_____

_____

What was the most challenging obstacle you overcame together?

_____

_____

_____

_____

_____

_____

What is something your spouse does that makes you laugh?

_____

_____

_____

_____

How does your spouse inspire you to be better? _____

_____

_____

_____

_____

_____

Do you share any inside jokes? _____

_____

_____

_____

_____

_____

What is one thing you know about your spouse that no one else

knows? _____

_____

_____

_____

DO YOU HAVE A
SPECIAL SONG? WHAT IS IT?

WHAT IS YOUR FAVORITE
ACTIVITY YOU DO TOGETHER?

WHEN YOU WAKE UP EACH MORNING, WHAT IS THE
FIRST THING YOU NOTICE ABOUT YOUR SPOUSE?

What qualities are most valuable when looking for a life partner? _____

_____

_____

_____

_____

_____

How do you keep a marriage relationship happy and healthy with a house full of kids? _____

_____

_____

_____

_____

_____

_____

_____

Have you been married more than once? If so, list each of your spouses' full names. _____

_____

_____

_____

_____

_____

_____

Have you been divorced? What did you learn from that experience?

_____

_____

_____

_____

_____

_____

_____

_____

Have you ever been widowed? What advice would you give to others

who are going through the same experience? _____

_____

_____

_____

_____

_____

_____

_____

_____

Anything special or unique about your spouse or being married that you want to share? _____

_____

_____

_____

_____

_____

_____

_____

_____

_____

_____

_____

_____

_____

_____

_____

_____

_____

_____

_____

SKETCHES

Can you draw or just doodle?
Use these pages to sketch something you've learned to draw.

Together

we make a

FAMILY.

A FAMILY OF MY OWN

CHILD'S NAME	BIRTHDATE & BIRTHPLACE
CHILD'S NAME	BIRTHDATE & BIRTHPLACE
CHILD'S NAME	BIRTHDATE & BIRTHPLACE
CHILD'S NAME	BIRTHDATE & BIRTHPLACE
CHILD'S NAME	BIRTHDATE & BIRTHPLACE
CHILD'S NAME	BIRTHDATE & BIRTHPLACE
CHILD'S NAME	BIRTHDATE & BIRTHPLACE
CHILD'S NAME	BIRTHDATE & BIRTHPLACE
CHILD'S NAME	BIRTHDATE & BIRTHPLACE

What is the best thing about raising a child? _____

_____
_____
_____
_____
_____
_____
_____
_____
_____
_____

What is the hardest thing? _____

_____
_____
_____
_____
_____
_____
_____
_____
_____

Are all of your children your biological offspring? _____

_____

_____

Are any adopted? _____

_____

_____

_____

_____

How did you react when you found out you would become a parent

for the first time? _____

_____

_____

_____

_____

_____

_____

_____

_____

_____

_____

_____

_____

Who decided on the name for each child? _____

_____

_____

_____

_____

How many kids did you want when you first got married?

_____

_____

_____

How many did you have in the end? _____

_____

_____

_____

_____

What was the most challenging time of parenthood for you?

Life with a newborn, a toddler, a school-aged child, a teenager, or an

adult? _____

_____

_____

_____

_____

_____

_____

_____

HOW DID YOU DISCIPLINE
YOUR CHILDREN?

HOW DID YOU MANAGE YOUR
CHILDREN'S HOMEWORK?

WHERE DID YOU GO FOR FAMILY VACATIONS?

Do you have a family motto? What is it?

_____

_____

_____

_____

_____

_____

What has brought you the most joy as a parent? _____

_____

_____

_____

_____

_____

_____

_____

_____

_____

_____

_____

_____

_____

What significant illnesses have you had to deal with as a family?

_____
_____
_____
_____
_____
_____

What is a trait your child or children have that you wish you possessed? _____

_____
_____
_____
_____
_____
_____

Which child is most like you? In what way? _____

_____
_____
_____
_____
_____
_____
_____

What activities do you enjoy doing with your family?

_____

_____

_____

_____

_____

How did you balance the demands of work with family time?

_____

_____

_____

_____

_____

How are chores divided between the males and females in

your family? _____

_____

_____

_____

_____

_____

_____

_____

_____

_____

_____

What are some thoughtful things your children have done for you
over the years?

How did you teach your children what is essential in life?

WHAT ADVICE WOULD
YOU GIVE YOUR KIDS
ABOUT RAISING CHILDREN?

What's the craziest thing one of your kids ever did?

_____

_____

_____

_____

_____

_____

_____

_____

_____

How has being a parent changed you? _____

_____

_____

_____

_____

_____

_____

_____

_____

_____

You are never
too old to set
another goal or
to dream a

NEW DREAM.

NOW THAT THE
KIDS ARE GROWN

What is a typical day like for you now? _____

_____

_____

_____

_____

_____

_____

_____

How is it different from when you were younger?

_____

_____

_____

_____

_____

_____

_____

What is the best part of being an empty nester? _____

_____

_____

_____

_____

_____

What is something you would like to do now that the kids are grown?

_____

_____

_____

_____

_____

_____

What did you love about having children in your home? _____

_____

_____

_____

_____

_____

WHAT IS THE WORST
THING ABOUT LIVING
WITHOUT THE KIDS?

IF YOU COULD GO BACK IN TIME AND DO
SOMETHING DIFFERENTLY, WHAT WOULD IT BE?

Do you have any grandkids? How many?

_____

_____

_____

What do you like to do with your free time? _____

_____

_____

_____

_____

_____

_____

What is a goal you are currently pursuing? _____

_____

_____

_____

_____

_____

_____

_____

_____

At what age do you plan on retiring? _____

_____

_____

If you could live anywhere, where would it be? _____

_____

_____

_____

What new hobbies have you started lately? _____

_____

_____

_____

_____

Do you have any physical challenges? _____

_____

_____

_____

_____

What are you looking forward to as you grow old together?

_____

_____

_____

_____

_____

PLACES I HAVE CALLED HOME

Where I have lived throughout my childhood life.

(List the city/state/country & dates)

PLACES I HAVE CALLED HOME

Where I have lived throughout my adult life.

(List the city/state/country & dates)

He takes us as
we are and makes us
MORE than we
EVER
IMAGINED.

ALL ABOUT ME

How tall are you? _____

_____

What sports have you played throughout your life?

_____

_____

_____

_____

_____

_____

_____

What kind of music do you like? _____

_____

_____

_____

_____

_____

_____

If you could change something about yourself physically, what would it be? _____

_____

_____

_____

_____

What is something most people don't know about you?

_____

_____

_____

_____

_____

Are you right- or left-handed? _____

_____

_____

Do you have a tattoo? What is it and where is it located?

_____

_____

_____

_____

_____

_____

_____

What is your zodiac sign? _____

_____

If you could have a superpower, what would it be? _____

_____

_____

_____

What makes you laugh? _____

_____

_____

_____

_____

_____

_____

Which languages do you speak? _____

_____

_____

_____

_____

_____

WHAT MOTIVATES YOU?

Have you ever snow- or water-skied?_____

_____

_____

_____

What kinds of things do you like to make? _____

_____

_____

_____

Which professional/amateur team do you follow? _____

_____

_____

_____

Have you ever been in an accident? What happened?

Which bones have you broken?

What are the worst injuries you have endured?

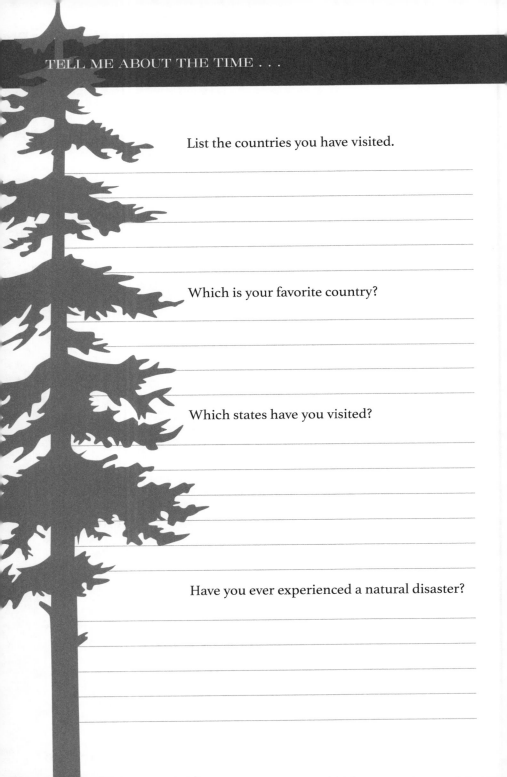

List the countries you have visited.

Which is your favorite country?

Which states have you visited?

Have you ever experienced a natural disaster?

List the musical instruments you play. _____

_____

_____

_____

_____

_____

What do you like to do in your spare time? _____

_____

_____

_____

_____

_____

_____

_____

_____

If you received a gift of a billion dollars, how would you spend it?

_____

_____

_____

_____

_____

_____

_____

Do you have any allergies? _____

_____

_____

_____

Have you ever ridden a horse? _____

_____

_____

In times of trouble in your life, who did you turn to for advice or help?

_____

_____

_____

_____

_____

_____

Have you ever had a serious illness? _____

_____

_____

_____

_____

_____

What is one of the craziest things you have ever done? _____

_____

_____

_____

_____

_____

Do you like to dance? _____

_____

_____

_____

What is something you feel you do well? _____

_____

_____

_____

_____

_____

What hobbies do you enjoy? _____

_____

_____

_____

_____

_____

Do you know how to swim? _____

_____

Which Olympic event do you favor? _____

_____

_____

_____

_____

_____

_____

Have you ever been lost? _____

_____

_____

_____

_____

_____

_____

_____

_____

Which political party do you support? _____

_____

_____

_____

_____

_____

What is a little-known skill or talent you have?

_____

_____

_____

_____

Can you ride a bike? _____

_____

What is something you have done that you regret?

_____

_____

_____

_____

_____

_____

What is an interesting fact most people wouldn't know
about you? _____

_____

_____

_____

_____

_____

Which item do you own or possess that is of greatest value to you?

_____

_____

_____

_____

_____

_____

What is something you collect that is meaningful to you?

_____

_____

_____

_____

What is the scariest thing you have ever done? _____

_____

_____

_____

_____

_____

_____

_____

_____

Share something you are afraid of and why. _____

_____

_____

_____

_____

_____

_____

_____

_____

_____

_____

What is the most embarrassing thing that has ever happened to you?

_____

_____

_____   _____

A FEW OF MY
FAVORITE THINGS

Candy

Fragrance

Movie

Sport to participate in

Sport to watch

Song _____

Animal _____

Outside activity _____

Day of the week _____

Soda

Book

Meal

Food to cook _____

Local place to go _____

Place to shop _____

Person to spend time with _____

Actor/Actress _____

Season of the Year _____

Fruit & vegetable

Way to relax

Vacation spot

Food to eat

Car/Truck _____

Cartoon _____

TV Show _____

Soda _____

Drink

Flower

Hymn

Pet

Color

Book _____

Fast food restaurant _____

Fine dining restaurant _____

The world is full
of good people.
If you can't find one,
BE ONE.

THINGS THAT MATTER

Which charitable organizations have you supported?

_____

_____

_____

_____

_____

Do you remember a time when you helped someone less

fortunate? What happened? _____

_____

_____

_____

_____

_____

_____

_____

_____

_____

_____

List the people who have had the most significant impact on your life
(family members, coaches, mentors, leaders, friends, etc.). Why?

_____

_____

_____

_____

_____

_____

_____

_____

_____

_____

_____

_____

_____

_____

_____

_____

_____

_____

_____

_____

_____

WHAT ADVICE WOULD
YOU GIVE TO THOSE WHO
HAVE MADE BAD
DECISIONS IN THEIR LIVES?

SHARE ONE CHALLENGING PROBLEM YOU HAVE
FACED AND HOW YOU OVERCAME IT.

Was there ever a time when you doubted yourself or your worth?

_____

_____

_____

_____

_____

_____

_____

_____

_____

How did you rebuild your confidence and self-esteem?

_____

_____

_____

_____

_____

_____

_____

_____

_____

_____

_____

What is something you took for granted in the past that is special to you now?

In what ways has the world changed over your lifetime?

SHINE

so that through

you, others can

SEE HIM.

BELIEFS & FAITH

What was your religion while growing up?

_____

_____

_____

Which specific church or churches did you attend as a child?

_____

_____

_____

_____

_____

Does your early religious upbringing align with your
spiritual beliefs now? _____

_____

_____

_____

_____

_____

_____

_____

Is prayer an essential part of your life? _____

_____

_____

_____

If you pray, what do you find yourself praying for most often?

_____

_____

_____

_____

_____

_____

_____

Do you remember a specific circumstance when you received

an answer to prayer? _____

_____

_____

_____

_____

_____

_____

_____

_____

_____

_____

Do you believe in God? _____

_____

_____

_____

_____

Do you believe in life after death? _____

_____

_____

_____

_____

_____

Are you afraid of dying? _____

_____

_____

_____

_____

In which positions have you served in your church? ____

_____

_____

_____

_____

_____

_____

HAVE YOU EVER LOST
A LOVED ONE?

WHO HAVE YOU LOST AND HOW
DID IT MAKE YOU FEEL?

Have you served a mission for your church? If so, where did you
serve, and when did you fill this assignment? _____

_____

_____

_____

_____

_____

_____

What is a favorite scripture or inspirational thought that has
influenced you? _____

_____

_____

_____

_____

_____

_____

What do you read or study to strengthen your faith? _____

_____

_____

_____

_____

_____

_____

Have you ever changed religions? _____

_____

_____

_____

_____

What does Jesus Christ mean to you? If you are not
Christian, what other deity is significant to you and why?

_____

_____

_____

_____

_____

_____

_____

_____

_____

_____

_____

_____

_____

_____

_____

_____

_____

_____

What would you like to share with your children and grandchildren about your faith?

How has a belief in God helped you overcome adversity and trials in your life?

How has your faith been strengthened through the years?

_____

_____

_____

_____

_____

_____

_____

_____

How does your faith help you in your day-to-day life?

_____

_____

_____

_____

_____

_____

_____

_____

_____

What do you feel is our purpose in life?

Anything special or unique about your beliefs or faith that you want
to share or expand on? _____

_____

_____

_____

_____

_____

_____

_____

_____

_____

_____

_____

_____

_____

_____

_____

_____

_____

_____

_____

_____

_____

WHAT I VALUE MOST

Words that describe what is most important to me.

NEVER BE AFRAID

to try something new.
Life gets boring when you
stay within the limits
of what you already know.

HAVE YOU EVER?

YES	NO	
☐	☐	FIRED A GUN?
☐	☐	TRIED ARCHERY?
☐	☐	HUNTED GAME?
☐	☐	GONE FISHING?
☐	☐	SWAM IN A RIVER?
☐	☐	GONE SKIING OR SNOWBOARDING?
☐	☐	TRIED SCUBA DIVING?
☐	☐	GONE SKY DIVING?
☐	☐	MILKED A COW?
☐	☐	ATTENDED SUMMER CAMP?
☐	☐	COMPETED IN A COMPETITION?
☐	☐	WON A MEDAL OR RIBBON?
☐	☐	BEEN ON TV?
☐	☐	TOURED ANOTHER COUNTRY?
☐	☐	LIVED ABROAD?

YES NO

☐	☐	SWAM WITH DOLPHINS?
☐	☐	WENT KAYAKING?
☐	☐	EATEN FROG LEGS?
☐	☐	HAD A SECRET ADMIRER?
☐	☐	TRAVELED BY TRAIN?
☐	☐	OWNED A REPTILE?
☐	☐	SLEPT UNDER THE STARS?
☐	☐	BEEN DUMPED?
☐	☐	DUMPED SOMEONE?
☐	☐	ICE SKATED?
☐	☐	HAD TO GET STITCHES?
☐	☐	BEEN ARRESTED?
☐	☐	GOTTEN A TICKET?
☐	☐	BEEN ON THE RADIO?
☐	☐	FALLEN IN LOVE AT FIRST SIGHT?
☐	☐	RECEIVED A PRESENT YOU HATED?
☐	☐	SLEPT IN A TENT?
☐	☐	FELT AN EARTHQUAKE?
☐	☐	RIDDEN A MOTORCYCLE?
☐	☐	HITCHHIKED?

YES   NO

☐   ☐   VISITED A FORTUNE TELLER?

☐   ☐   ACTED ON STAGE?

☐   ☐   WON ANYTHING?

☐   ☐   BEEN STUNG BY A BEE?

☐   ☐   MADE A YOUTUBE VIDEO?

☐   ☐   SEEN A GHOST?

☐   ☐   SEEN A UFO?

☐   ☐   BEEN TO DISNEYLAND?

☐   ☐   HAD BRACES?

☐   ☐   SUNG KARAOKE?

☐   ☐   BEEN IN AN AMBULANCE?

☐   ☐   RIDDEN IN A HELICOPTER?

☐   ☐   BEEN IN A FIRETRUCK?

☐   ☐   GOTTEN ANYTHING PIERCED?

☐   ☐   HAD SURGERY?

☐   ☐   GIVEN MONEY TO THE HOMELESS?

☐   ☐   CUT YOUR OWN HAIR?

☐   ☐   SWAM IN THE OCEAN?

☐   ☐   GONE SURFING?

☐   ☐   EATEN A BUG?

Only look back
to see how far
YOU'VE COME.

WHEN ALL IS
SAID & DONE

What do you want your spouse to remember when you are

gone? _____

_____

_____

_____

_____

_____

_____

_____

_____

_____

_____

_____

_____

_____

_____

_____

_____

_____

_____

What was the happiest time in your life? _____

_____

_____

_____

_____

_____

_____

_____

_____

_____

_____

What was the saddest? _____

_____

_____

_____

_____

_____

_____

_____

_____

What family values do you hope your children will continue for
generations in the future?

_____

_____

_____

_____

_____

_____

_____

_____

_____

_____

_____

_____

_____

_____

_____

_____

_____

_____

Do you have a living trust or will? _____

_____

_____

_____

_____

Is your estate planning complete? _____

_____

_____

_____

_____

_____

Where do you keep important documents and keepsakes?

_____

_____

_____

_____

_____

_____

_____

_____

_____

_____

_____

_____

What unique heirlooms are cherished by your family?

Where are they now? _____

_____

_____

_____

_____

_____

_____

_____

_____

What do you wish most for your children? _____

_____

_____

_____

_____

_____

_____

_____

_____

_____

_____

_____

WHAT ARE YOU DOING
TODAY TO BUILD A LEGACY THAT
YOU WANT TO LEAVE BEHIND?

If you could share one message with your children and grandchildren that would remain in their hearts and minds forever, what would it be?

_____

_____

_____

_____

_____

_____

_____

_____

_____

_____

_____

_____

_____

_____

_____

_____

_____

_____

_____

_____

What do you want people to remember about you?

You never know the

VALUE

of a moment until

it becomes a

MEMORY.

I DON'T WANT
TO FORGET

Use these pages to share other thoughts, stories, or experiences that have come to mind and you want to remember.

GRANDPA, TELL ME
ABOUT THE TIME . . .